From
Rejection
to
Rejoicing

VELMA SHANKS

INKWATER
PRESS

www.inkwaterpress.com

ISBN 1-59299-140-8

Publisher: Inkwater Press

Printed in the U.S.A.

$\mathcal{I}$ dedicate this book to my mother, Vera M. Shanks. You are an exemplary example of a godly woman. Thank you for being the wind beneath my wings. I love you.

Table of Contents

Acknowledgements

First and foremost all Praise and Honor to my Lord and Savior Jesus Christ.

To my pastor, Elder Andre' Landers: This book is in print because of the messages you preach that inspires me to walk in every promise that the Lord has given to me.

To Dr. Donnie N. McGriff: Bishop, thank you for pushing me to reach dimensions in my ministry that I never thought I would attain. You trained and prepared me for such a time as this.

To my Armor Bearer, Cheri Pope: I can't even put into words what you mean to me. I know that God has only loaned you to me for a season. I want you to know that when you are behind me, supporting me and uplifting my arms, what I actually feel is the strength and power of God Himself upholding me. May God richly bless you and the ministry He is yet unfolding for you.

To Tracey Ealy and Shirley Kennedy, your grammar skills are the bomb!

I love you all.

Foreword

Within the pages of this book lies a familiar journey for many who will read it. A journey that begins with pain, confusion and brokenness. However, later in this journey you will find hope, healing, and restoration.

This author's story is at times riveting but completely relevant to the challenges both men and women experience today. "From Rejection to Rejoicing" is a testimony of God's ability to facilitate complete wholeness despite a past filled with continual rejection. It reminds us that our ultimate goal should be to develop real intimacy with God - For in such lies no rejection!

Read this Book slowly and allow God to minister to you from its pages as he reminds you that he wants to turn your mess into a message, and instead of remaining a victim, allow your pain to be the springboard which propels you into your divine destiny.

Pastor Daryl W. Tilghman
Restoration Ministries
San Diego, GA

Endorsement

Evangelist Velma Shanks has been a student of the Word God for many years. She is an anointed woman of God, having the privilege of speaking in conferences, conducting seminars in singles retreats, ministering in the state of California in powerful prophetic revivals.

Therefore, the work that you are about to read was not done overnight. It is through divine inspiration that Evangelist Shanks has taken pen and paper with a compilation of many hours of study, ministering, counseling, revelation, illumination, and personal experience.

As a former member of Christ Temple Apostolic Church, an International Ministry, where I'm the Pastor. I witnessed the power and anointing of God evident in her life. She has a unique ability to touch women where they are hurting as you will witness through this book.

I give glory and honor to God for blessing Evangelist Shanks to become an anointed writer with the ability to enlighten others by way of the printed page. This is a must read book, all that read it will be blessed as she shares with you some spiritual insight and personal experiences God has given her through her journey, **"From Rejection to Rejoicing."**

Dr. Donnie N. McGriff
Pastor/Founder Christ Temple Apostolic Church
President/International Apostolic University
Bishop/Christ Temple International Ministries

Preface

We recently hosted a Singles' Conference at my church. It was through this conference that God birthed this book. I taught a seminar by the same title: "From Rejection to Rejoicing." During this seminar the power of God came in the room in such a way that He even surprised me. I was about three-fourths of the way through the class when the women began to cry and call out to God for their healing. God moved that day beyond my greatest expectations. I knew the body of Christ, especially the women of Christ, was suffering with the spirit of rejection, but I had no idea to what degree until that day. When I went home that evening, God spoke to me and said to put my experiences that brought about this seminar into a book. He told me in the same way that He healed those women that attended my seminar, He would heal each person who read this book and applied the steps that moved me from rejection to rejoicing.

The following Tuesday I received e-mail from one of the attendees of the seminar. I have included it in this chapter as a testimony to the healing that God had done and will do through my experiences you are about to read.

As you read this book, read it with an open heart. Allow God to show you areas in your life that are similar to mine. Areas where rejection has occurred and the pain you are still carrying because of it. As you open yourself up, you will begin to feel the power and anointing of God; go to those areas that you thought were buried. Don't be afraid to go through the process, the process …"From Rejection to Rejoicing."

Here is the e-mail:

"Words cannot express the gratitude I feel in my soul, heart, and mind. I want to thank you again for allowing God to use you in the way He does. Your willingness to yield to God is an asset to the ministry God is preparing you for and because of that, the people of God will be blessed beyond measure.

I just want to share with you what the Lord did for me in Room A. For the past ten years or so, I was being tormented by a spirit that would taunt me about my physical appearance and my lack of male admirers and would remind me of all my past failures in relationships. I would rebuke it and intensify my study and prayer time so that the Spirit of the Lord could help me keep my mind and focus on God and not on my vacancies. Sometimes, I would find myself watching certain shows and movies and then I would have to battle off the desires they would provoke as I was sent into a heavy spirit of depression that would follow.

This went on and on for quite some time. I would fight and come up with the victory and then fall again, finding myself in this vicious cycle. The Lord would give me things to do to help keep my sanity and my spirit free. I would follow this regimen for a time and sometimes I would fall off the wagon.

When God filled me with His Spirit in 1993, I thought after having such an awesome encounter with the Lord that I had overcome and conquered this thing for good. But every time I would have a mountain top experience with the Lord, I would come down battling this thing again. I had no idea what the cause of this was until Saturday, September 30 in Room A.

While in the session 'From Rejection to Rejoicing' the Lord ministered to me in a dynamic and awesome way. I was not expecting anything like this. I didn't know I needed something like this to happen in my life. I thought I was cool. But as you ministered and the Spirit of the Lord and His anointing was thick in the room, the Lord began to speak to me.

I was dealing with a lack of confidence in my ability to effectively minister to adults. The youth accepted me fine but, because of my insecurities about what people thought of me, I did not know how to conduct myself right around older people.

But as you laid hands on me and said, 'I rebuke the spirit of rejection off your life. This is your season, go forth in the power of the Lord.'

You then said, 'Don't change who you are; God made you and He made you just the way He wanted you.' Suddenly I felt the dam break! A flood of emotion and release overtook me. I heard the voice of the Lord say, "I am going into your past and healing you from all the hurts and pain that you received from the rejections in your life." Then a video started playing in my mind, the Lord was showing me all the incidents in my life where rejection had occurred and the baggage that came with it. He showed me the manifested actions, habits and problems that came because of rejection. Then the Lord said, 'Be healed and be tormented no more.'

Introduction

Rejoice In The Face Of Rejection?

How do you face rejection and still rejoice? Is it possible for you to find joy when you're left to feel as though you are not good enough, not worthy enough, not attractive enough or not intelligent enough? The answer is "Yes." You could have just been told you are not the one and still hold your head high and say hallelujah anyhow!

Rejection is defined as: "to throw back, repulse, to spew out to refuse to accept." *Repulse* is defined as "to repel by discourtesy, coldness or denial." When a person is rejected it is usually done in a cold, discourteous manner by someone they love.

Everyone desires to be loved, when we are betrayed by the one we thought loved us rejection enters. If rejection is not dealt with, it will take root in your flesh and conceive unwanted off-spring. Rejection that is not dealt with will produce any one of the following, if not all: jealousy, envy, hatred, bitterness, malice, contempt, low self esteem, depression, and ultimately, it can lead to suicide.

One who has been rejected often feels the need to validate their self-worth to others; this person tends to suffer from a lack of appropriate affirmation. This quest for validation is often sexualized.

The Process

There is a process in moving from rejection to rejoicing, but it is not a pleasant one. It will take going all the way back to the time when the initial seed of rejection was planted and digging it up without leaving any roots remaining. That means digging past every hurt, every pain, every disappointment, every betrayal, and every broken dream and shattered vision. It will mean digging until you find the beginning of the root that caused such a horrible monster to grow in your life. Laying an ax at the root will destroy the possibility of recurring growth.

I can remember when rejection was first planted in my life…

Chapter 1

How the Seed was Planted

I grew up in a home that wasn't filled with hugs and kisses and kind words. In fact, there wasn't much communication at all. I never saw mom and dad showing affection toward one another. I do, however, remember the arguments. My father often wouldn't come home from work until late in the evening (because my father would often come home so late, we really never developed a relationship with dad).

We were all in bed, supposed to be asleep, but I was awake and could hear the verbal blows that my parents were tossing back and forth. Then I would hear my mother say, "Get out. I don't want you here anymore." Or I would hear my father say, "I'm leaving." I was about seven years old when I remember the first instance. I was petrified, laying there in my bed thinking when I got up that morning my daddy was not going to be there and I would never see him again. Why didn't he want to stay with us? Why would he leave us? He didn't love us. Enter rejection. I would just lay in the bed and cry. It scared me to think about life without my dad. That same scene was repeated throughout my childhood.

I know my mother loved us. She made sure we had everything we needed and most of what we wanted, even if that meant dealing with dad about the money issue later. At the time though, I really wanted a part of her that she just didn't have to give – the affection.

My mother was married at the age of 16. She went from raising her brothers and sisters while her mother was at work, into a marriage with a man who was dealing with issues himself. My mother did not get the love and affection she needed while she was growing up, so she did not know how to show affection to her own children.

I was determined that this generational curse was not going to be carried to my children. I tell my son every day how much I love him. I am flooded with hugs and kisses from my son constantly. Sometimes I have to tell him, "Okay. Okay, Isaiah, that's enough." As I am writing, he's just come up to me at the computer and given me a hug and kiss. I wouldn't trade it for the world.

My Upbringing...

I was a "military brat." My father was in the Air Force, which meant we were constantly on the go. Just as we would get settled in one state, he would have orders to move again. The moves came in intervals of about every other year. We never stayed in one place longer than two years. I was always the new kid in the class. Being new and sometimes coming in the middle of the school year caused me to be very shy. I would come into a class in which everyone else already knew each other and nobody knew me. I would try to make myself sick, faking symptoms, just so they would send me home. I felt left out and out of place most of the time...rejection began to be watered.

That seed of rejection had been planted and began to be watered by different situations throughout my life. As I reached my pre-teen years I began to take note of my looks. I was the only one in my family that wore glasses and was teased by my other siblings. Nothing real mean, just the usual four-eyes jokes. But, to a child who already was insecure, it just watered the seed of rejection that had already been planted.

By the time I reached the seventh grade, I was so insecure about my looks that I would wear the glasses out of the house, but by the time I got to school, they were tucked away somewhere until it was time to go home again

My glasses were not ordinary glasses because I didn't have ordinary vision. One of my eyes was stronger than the other and the weaker eye was also a lazy eye, which meant I could not control its direction. When I would look at someone if I did not have my glasses on, they would constantly turn to look over their shoulder to see who I was looking at (Leah, in the story of Jacob, had nothing on my eyes).

Wearing the glasses was just as bad because in the '70s they had not yet created the high tech plastic they make the lenses out of now and because one of my eyes was weaker than the other, that meant one lens was thicker than the other, and back then they made the lenses out of glass. Yes, you guessed it: the glass was so heavy on one side that my glasses would often lean to that side. I was messed up if I wore them and messed up if I didn't…rejection continued to be watered. Thank God for contacts! Hallelujah!

My First Love

During the summer of my fourteenth birthday, just before beginning the ninth grade, I went to a teen dance with my older sister. I met an "older" boy there, Sam. Sam was in the eleventh grade and to a young, naive girl who was just looking to be loved, he was the one who filled every empty space in my heart. We exchanged phone numbers and began to see each other. My mother and father were both working. They never took the time to inquire, who is this young man coming around? They never asked "how old is he?" "Where does he live?" "What does he want with you?" So, before long, I fell head over heels in love with Sam. I would do anything for him. He loved me. Or so he said. Sam became my first at everything. I was devastated when I found out he really didn't love me at all. He was a young man with just one goal and that was to get what he could out of an inexperienced young girl. When the relationship ended, I was left wounded and bleeding from rejection.

Sam had never stopped seeing his ex-girlfriend and actually got engaged while we were still seeing each other. Sue, Sam, and I had a confrontation, and Sam denied everything about our relationship right in front of me. He called me crazy, and every other word you can think of that would tear down a young lady's character. I was devastated. How could my first love treat me this way? I gave him all I had. Now he took all I had left, my dignity. I was left with wounds that would take years to heal…rejection continued to be watered.

When Jesus Found Me…

My mother raised us in church. However, by the time I was in the eleventh grade, we were not members of a particular church. We would be the ones that you would see twice a year, on Easter and Mother's day. Well, maybe Christmas too. We were living in Tacoma, Washington at this time. We had moved there in 1974 and I remained in Tacoma until 1987, the longest time I ever spent in one place during my adolescent years, so that is where I consider home.

In 1982, I was in eleventh grade at the time, Jesus found me. I had a male friend whom I was interested in that invited me to his church. I joined this church and became very involved. Singing in the choir and attending Bible study and Sunday school. It was during my time at this church that God began to start the process of healing. The process, which was very painful, involved a few more instances that caused rejection to continue to be watered.

Chapter 2

The Seed Continued to Grow

I was filled with the Holy Spirit in February of 1983. I was now a senior in high school. I was a varsity cheerleader at the time and felt God's call to sanctify myself. I quit cheerleading before the school year was over to much of the squad's surprise. I tried to explain the best way I could. "God has saved me and He told me to give cheerleading up." Not that being a cheerleader was wrong, but my motives were wrong. You see, being a cheerleader had become a crutch for me. I had a low self-image and when I was in uniform and had the attention on me, I felt like I was somebody. God wanted me to get to the place where I knew I was somebody, not because of what I was, but because of *whose* I was. I belonged to the King. God had to teach me that I was a queen and He loved me just the way I was – but too much to let me remain that way. I graduated from high school in June of the same year.

Rejection Waiting in the Wings

Not long after graduation, while attending a revival with my church, a man whom I had known in passing from the church approached me and we began talking. He was so easy to talk to. He was a bit older than I was, although I never did find out his exact age. He was a deacon in the church, and I was flattered that he took interest in me. I had not really had a relationship with my father, as we were always in bed by the time he would come home from work. I began to see Deacon James as a father figure. Somewhere along the course of time, however, I developed an attraction for James. We would spend hours on the phone, and I would visit him at his house. Again, he was older, so he owned his own home. James was kind to me. I was able to be myself with him. I shared every secret, every pain and every joy. I would not make decisions without first asking James what he thought. The relationship or "friendship," as he would call it, between James and I continued for about seven years. It was a secret, though, to most of the people at church. I think it was because James knew how old I was, and he knew the age difference would not be accepted by many. Again, I did not know James' age. I found out years later that James was about 17 years my senior. That would have put me at 18 years of age dealing with a man about 35 or 36 years old. Rejection had a field day in this relationship.

Rude Awakening

One night I called James. It was New Year's Eve and we had returned home from our watch night service at church. James answered the phone and as he was putting the receiver to his ear, he was still talking to whoever was at his house. I heard a female voice through the phone. Who was at James' house? Why would he have another woman over there instead of me? James was cold and told me he had company and could not talk.

I was about 20 years old at the time and really did not know how to handle the pain I was feeling. I was sick to my stomach thinking about what James might be doing with his newfound friend. I got in my parents' car, it was about 3:00 a.m. by this time, and went to James' house. I tried to peek though the window. I just wanted to know who it was. I could not see through my tears and his stupid curtains.

James was very meticulous about how he kept his house and yard. He had just landscaped his yard very nicely with flowers and plants lining the sidewalk. I'm sure he was quite surprised when he left to escort his lady friend to her car to see his sidewalk filled with the flowers and plants that I had pulled up in my rage of rejection.

James tried to get me to understand that whatever we had was over. He didn't want to be my friend any longer.

My parents were also going through a divorce at the time. They finally split after 27 years of marriage. I did not know how to deal with the emotions that were going through my heart.

One morning I was home alone and decided I was going to get James' attention by taking some pills. I really did not want to kill myself; I just wanted him to say " Oh, poor Velma, I really hurt her. I really do love her," WRONG! What I did get was a trip to the hospital and about four hours of dry heaving from the medication I had to take to pump my stomach. Oh, and not to forget the visit with the psychiatrist. Well, after about an hour with the doctor, they decided I wasn't crazy. I was just a young lady who was carrying a lot of pain and was crying out for some love and attention. The healing was about to begin.

Chapter 3

The Healing Was About to Begin

*I*n 1987 God allowed me to get hired by Continental Airlines as a flight attendant. I believe He knew I had to get as far away from James as I could to really get over the relationship.

As a flight attendant, God allowed me to see places like Japan, Australia, New Zealand, Tahiti, Guam, and most of the United States. I had a job that took me to a new city and sometimes a new country every week. It was during this time that the healing process began. I would be in my hotel room on a layover (each crew member had their own room) all by myself again. God had put me in a position where I had to be alone with myself, which caused me to get to know me. He slowly began to work on my self-esteem; I wasn't such a bad person to be alone with after all.

God began to do something in my spirit. He began to ignite a true love for Him. I would sleep with my Bible, studying late into the night. I wanted to know God in an intimate way.

When my flight schedule allowed me to attend church, The Holy Spirit would come into our services in mighty ways. There would even be times when my pastor could not preach. He would have an altar call and souls would come to give their lives to Jesus. I would find myself in the Spirit under pews, on the floor. Whatever it took, I wanted it; I just wanted to be saved and I wanted to be free!

God began to use me to minister to others even though I myself was still in the process of being healed. I would lay hands on the sick and they would be healed.

I remember praying once for a lady who had a bleeding ulcer. I just prayed a simple prayer and didn't think about it until sometime later. I saw the lady in service and asked her, "How are you feeling? How is your ulcer?" To my surprise – yes, my surprise – even though I had prayed for her healing I had never really witnessed God actually performing a miracle right before me. The lady said, "The ulcer is gone, I no longer have any pain anymore." I began to cry and praise God right there.

God let me know through other instances of healing and deliverance that I had a special anointing on my life. I didn't know it then, but every rejection and every pain I had ever felt, and was yet to experience, was all in God's plan. ***The anointing*** ***is only released through a process of crushing and pressing.***

Chapter 4

The Process of Crushing and Pressing...

This is a very difficult chapter to do, but I have overcome by the blood of the lamb and by the word of my testimony. I have only told two or three people at the most of my experience in Tulsa, but God is leading me to briefly share it because God said, "You are not the only one this has happened to."

As you read this chapter please do not read it in judgment. If something like this has never happened to you, then you need to praise God. But believe me, this sort of thing is happening all over the country in the body of Christ.

In February of 1990 I accepted my call into the ministry. I was in the spirit worshiping and praising God during a service that a well-known Evangelist was preaching when I heard the call. God said " You are an Evangelist and I am calling you to preach my word." After a few seconds of warfare, (my flesh did not want to submit to what the spirit was saying), I said yes to the Lord and from that time on the process of crushing and pressing began.

I left Tacoma in August of 1990 to move to Tulsa to attend a well-known Bible College; it was then that I really got free from the soul tie I had developed with James. That soul tie was broken but little did I know I had a trap waiting for me in Tulsa.

While in Tulsa I attended a nationally known, high profile church and became involved in the ministry there. God used my experience at this church to crush the anointing out of me in such a way that I felt like David: "God, please don't take Your Spirit away from me."

I arrived in Tulsa in August of 1990, the Lord allowed to me find a job within 3 days (I quit the airlines to attend Bible college).

I was now in a city in which I knew no one. I left all my friends and family in Tacoma. I was so lonely. I remember praying and crying out to the Lord to fill the emptiness that I was feeling from being alone in a new city at 25 years of age, still very naive and trusting of most people. I believed if they were in the church, and especially a minister, they loved God as much as I did. If they loved God, surely they wouldn't hurt me, right? Wrong! Rejection thought it would really kill me this time.

I was faithful at my new church home. I worked on the altar team, in the youth ministry, and sang in the choir. There was a particular Elder at the church that you had to counsel with if you were interested in becoming licensed in the ministry through the church.

Elder Smith took special interest in me. He said he recognized the anointing of God on my life and wanted to mentor me in the ministry. He was married to a beautiful woman, so I had no idea that the anointing was not the only thing he recognized in me.

Elder Smith would counsel me weekly. He was so easy to talk to. I opened up to him and shared about my past hurts, disappointments, and achievements.

Soon, I began to receive phone calls at my home. He said he was calling "just to check on me," knowing I was in a new city by myself. I thought it was so nice that this anointed man of God – he really had an anointing on his life – took the time to see about me and make sure I was doing okay. The calls became more frequent until I began to look for and expected him to call every night about 10:00 p.m. He would spend an hour or two each evening "ministering to me." Single women listen to me. There is no reason, I don't care what he says, that a married man should be calling you to "minister" and to check on you, especially at 10:00 in the evening. If it is taking place, **Stop it now**; it is a **TRAP**! (Psalms 91:1-3) *He who dwells in the secret place of the Most High shall abide under the shadow of the Almighty. I will say of the Lord, "He is my refuge and my fortress; my God in Him I will trust." Surely He shall deliver **you** from the **snare** of the fowler and from the perilous pestilence.* Tell him you appreciate his concern and ask him where his wife is. Ask him if she knows if he is calling you. Tell him if he doesn't lose your number you will tell his wife (Believe me, the phone calls will cease.)

The phone calls continued and then he began to call in the daytime also. He was on staff at the church, so he would call from his office.

One day he called and asked where my mailbox was located at home (he already knew where I lived from previous conversations, although he had never been to my house). I told him my mailbox was right at my door, and then I asked him why he wanted to know. He said he picked up a card to encourage me and wanted to drop it in my mailbox. I told him if he was going to drop it in my box, he may as well hand it to me because he would be at my door anyway. He came over that day to "bring me the card." Again, there is no way that a married man, especially an Elder, had any business at single woman's home. Male ministers, if you really are concerned for a female member, send one of the female ministers to check on her or at least take one with you. **Stop using the ministry to fulfill your flesh**. You know you are not really that concerned about that young lady. Your flesh is on fire and if you don't nip it in the bud now, you will find yourself in hell burning with the rest of the devil's imps. I'm not trying to hurt anyone; I'm just sick of the body of Christ being spiritually raped by wolves dressed in sheep's clothing!

So here I was with Elder Smith in my home. There had been about two months of communication between Elder Smith and myself. A sister at the church who had befriended me tried to warn me. She told me she noticed the way he would watch me at church and that he had an ulterior motive. I told her she was making more of it than what was really there. I did not want to hear her warnings. By this time I had gotten used to the attention, deception and denial had already crept in.

Elder Smith dropped the card off and left that day without incident. There were more visits to come though. He would find reasons to stop by. "I picked up a plant for you to brighten your apartment." " I just want to come by and check on you."

On one of these visits Elder Smith said the Lord and been dealing with him about me and sent him to minister to me.

Elder Smith began to tell me that God wanted me to be healed in the area of men. He said in the past men had always used me to get what they wanted and never really cared about me. He said God sent him to show me that all men are not that way. He said that when he looked at me, he saw my soul and not my body like other men did.

Elder Smith then said, "If you had nothing on right now I could look at you and not take advantage of you." Then he said, "I really wish I could prove it to you." I had a full-length mirror in my bedroom (my apartment was a junior apartment, which meant I did not have a door that closed off my bedroom from the living room; there was a separate room, but there was no partition). Elder Smith took me to the mirror and stood behind me and said, "Look at yourself. You are a beautiful young woman." He then said, "Take off your blouse and look at yourself the way God sees you." Before he left I had stood in that mirror with him standing behind me exposed from top to bottom so he could prove to me that "he was not interested in my body; he cared about Velma." Rejection was waiting in the wings with a grin on its face.

Elder Smith then helped me get dressed, gave me a hug and said, "God loves you and so do I." The spirit of deception had a death grip on me, and I actually believed that he was sent to minister to me. I mean, had he wanted to take advantage of me that would have been the most opportune time, right? I was fully unclothed and he didn't even touch me. He really did care about me and not my body. **Yeah, right!**

Within less than a week, Elder Smith found another reason to come to my house. This time, however, he said God wanted to really do some deep healing. He actually had me believing that what He was about to do would bring healing to me. He said it would be different with him because God sent him to minister to me.

When Elder Smith left that night after convincing me that having sex with him would bring "healing to me," I was left balled up in a fetal position, crying and feeling ashamed and dirty. He said he was different and he ended up doing the very thing he said he said he was sent to heal me from.

Then he had the nerve to ask me not to come to church for a while because he needed space and didn't know if he could handle seeing me at church. Rejection was in a full-blown laugh by this time. It knew it had me this time. I would never recover from this one. Rejection was wrong!

I did go to church that Sunday. Up until then I thought I'd been through some things, but the rejection I was about to be subjected to made everything else feel like child's play.

I'm Crushed and Now the Pressing...

Elder Smith would not even look in my direction at church. It was as if I never existed. This Elder that saw "the anointing on my life and wanted to mentor me in the ministry," now treated me like I was the black plague. He would not take any of my calls at the office. He acted as if he never knew me.

I looked into the face of rejection at church, every Wednesday and Sunday for the next six months. I would lay in my bed and cry while rocking myself to sleep at night. I was scared that God was going to withdraw His Spirit from me for what I had done. I read Psalms 51 until I could quote it word for word.....
(*Have mercy upon me, O God, according to Your loving-kindness; according to Your tender mercies, Blot out my transgressions. Wash me thoroughly from my iniquity, and cleanse me from my sin. For I acknowledge my transgressions, and my sin is ever before me. Against You, You only, have I sinned, and done this evil in Your sight - That I may be found just when You speak and blameless when You judge.....Purge me with hyssop, and I will be clean; wash me, and I shall be whiter than snow.....Create in me a clean heart and renew a steadfast spirit within me. Do not cast me away from your presence. And do not take Your Holy Spirit from me.*)

I begged God not to take His anointing away.

I stayed on the altar. Every time they had an altar call at church I was there right in the front of the crowd. I didn't care what people thought of me, I quit singing in the choir, working on the altar team and working with the youth. I needed God to restore me and I was not ashamed to lie on the altar until the process of healing was complete.

I never told the senior pastor of the church what had happened. I never told Elder Smith's wife. I didn't want revenge; I didn't even want Elder Smith. I just wanted to be saved!

I never intended to have an affair with a married man. I respect the institution of marriage, and the enemy knew that.

He had to disguise it in a form that I would not recognize. He masked it as "ministry." I had been tricked and deceived and the enemy thought what happened would destroy me. Rejection thought it had won this time, but God said not so. What the enemy meant for evil against me, God meant for my good. God came in and miraculously healed me from that experience and caused it to move me right into his will for my life. I left Tulsa about six months after the incident, completely healed. I could actually talk about what took place and not cry any longer (*You'll know you are healed when you can talk about what happened to you and it doesn't hurt any longer*).

Not only did I leave Tulsa completely healed, but also I left with the anointing oozing out of my life. I had been crushed to the point where I did not know if I was going to live or die. The rejection I faced in Tulsa came from the outside and the inside. I was not only dealing with the rejection from Elder Smith, but I was dealing with my own rejection. How could I be so stupid? Why didn't I see this coming? How could God still use me? Why would he still want to use me? I had been pressed beyond what most people could stand and did not lose my mind. There were times, though, that I actually thought I would.

Chapter 5

God's Will for My Life

God's will brought me to San Diego, California. I could no longer afford to live in Tulsa as the economy was not very good and the pay was much lower than what I was making as a flight attendant. I had family in

San Diego and they talked me into coming to California for a while. My plan was to return to Tulsa after I had paid off a few bills; that was not God's plan. I moved to San Diego in July of 1991. God's mercy and grace was shown to me in every way. Whatever job I applied for I would usually get. It was here that God completed the process of moving from rejection to rejoicing; however, not without one more blow from the enemy.

By 1993 God had begun to open doors for me in the ministry. Although I was a member of a church that did not recognize women ministers, God was sending me out to minister in other churches that did. Just at the peak of my ministry, rejection had set another trap for me…

I began to sing in a well-known community choir. God was blessing the ministry of the choir and myself. We would go out to minister and God would tell the director to use me to exhort and minister to the crowd. God would come in and bless the services mightily. I had an anointing on my life and that anointing would often draw men to me. What they were really attracted to was the anointing on my life, and not me as an individual. Inevitably, the relationships would go nowhere once they got to know me and realized I was human and the anointed woman they saw on the platform had shortcomings too.

In the summer of 1993 I walked right into another web of rejection. I had recently gotten out of a relationship and found a friend in the choir to talk to. He was in a relationship at the time but said he was unhappy. We started off as friends. We would share with one another, laugh with each other and talk about the Lord. It was a good friendship. I knew it was leading elsewhere but did not heed the word of the Lord. One night while praying, God lead me to Isaiah 52:11 *Depart! Depart! Go out from there, Touch no unclean thing…,(not that my friend was unclean but the relationship was unclean; it was* not *sanctioned by God)* I knew God was saying that this was not for me, but I was hard-headed. (We would save ourselves a lot of pain if we would just obey God when He speaks to us.) I didn't listen, however, and continued in the relationship in spite of God's warnings. Contrary to what most people believed, we were just friends for most of the relationship, strictly platonic. There was one night that he came over, and we both knew he should not have been there. One thing led to another and that night I conceived my son. God blessed me with a precious gift in spite of my sin. As I said earlier in the chapter, God had just begun to open doors in my ministry.

I was preaching revivals, exhorting at concerts, and teaching a young adult Bible study every Wednesday at my home church. How was I going to show my face in the city? Here I was, the one that was telling everyone else that you can live a holy and saved life, pregnant and about to be exposed before everyone. I knew I had to go to those I'd ministered to and repent. I remember thinking, Oh God, help me to do this.

Among the first people I told was my pastor at the time and his wife. I called my pastor and requested an appointment with him. We all were in the office; My pastor, his wife, me, and a friend who came for support. By the time I finished telling my pastor and his wife the story, we were all in tears. I repented before them and asked him to forgive me for the reproach I would bring upon the church. My pastor and his wife showed me unconditional love that day. He told me that God had forgiven me and so did they. I left the office with a sense of relief, but I knew I still had a couple of other groups to speak to.

I had to go to the young people who looked up to me as their leader and example and tell them that the very thing I was teaching them not to do, I myself had been caught in the trap. Again, when I finished telling my Bible study group the story, we were all in tears. Some hugged me and cried and some just sat there and cried. I knew some were crying because they loved me and knew I was hurting, but I also knew that some were crying because they looked up to me and I had let them down.

The last group I had to confront was the community choir I sang in. This was going to be difficult because my son's father, his then ex-girlfriend, and I all sang in this same choir together. By the time I went before them, however, the news had already hit the streets. This meeting was not a meeting to let them know what had happened, they had already gotten wind of that, but this meeting was for me to go before this group of people I prayed for, I ministered to, I laid hands on and exhorted in front of and ask them to forgive me for the reproach I would bring on the choir. It was one of the most difficult things I've ever had to do.

I looked in the faces of pure disgust. I knew many of them could not stand to see me standing before them, and many of them had to right to feel that way.

Before I told everyone else, I told John, the father of my baby. He took the news harder than I expected. Rejection was in the wings again. Remember the original relationship that watered the seed of rejection (Sam)? This relationship had similar issues. John had not stopped seeing who I thought was his ex-girlfriend. When I told him I was pregnant, he was preparing to tell me he didn't want to be with me any longer and that he realized it was Mary he actually loved. That was why he took the news so hard. I had no idea John still had feelings for Mary. Not only was I pregnant and unmarried, but I had also just been informed that the one I thought loved me, didn't.

John supported me throughout my pregnancy, but not without challenges. Following the birth of my son, John stuck to what he said concerning his feelings for Mary and within two years he and Mary were married.

God has allowed us through time to heal and there is a common respect that John, Mary and I have for one another.

Chapter 6

The Furnace of Affliction

*Y*es, I was rejected again, but this time God put me in a specific place until the process of moving from rejection to rejoicing was complete. The place God put me in was the refiner's fire. I was left in the fire for about five years.

A refiner's fire is a fire that one uses to purify precious metals. The procedure is used to free the object being tested of impurities or unwanted materials. It is used to make improvements in the product by introducing subtleties or distinctions. The fire in the furnace causes the impurities and unwanted materials to surface to the top of the metals being refined. Once the impurities have surfaced the refiner then scrapes the top of the barrel to remove the impurities from the matter. You may be in the furnace of affliction, the furnace of trials and tests, you may even be feeling as though you are literally being scraped by the cares of life. It's all a part of the process. Don't fight your test.

We each have distinctions that God has placed in us that differentiate you from me, your ministry from my ministry, your call from my call. The only way those subtleties or distinctions are going to surface is for us to be placed in the furnace of affliction. Isaiah 48:10 *"Behold I have refined you, but not as silver, I have refined you in the furnace of affliction."*

During this time in the furnace, God moved every friend I thought I had. Not only was I in the fire, but I was in it by myself. I was despised by some people because of the circumstances surrounding my pregnancy.

I would go to church services, most of the time by myself or just me and my baby, knowing that I would get sneered at and would be mocked and talked about.

I remember one particular service I attended. I was at a revival at the church that my son's father and his girlfriend attended. I was sitting in the service alone and there were two sisters sitting behind me. The two women knew the circumstances surrounding my ordeal and did not really care for me too much. While in the service, as the Prophet was speaking, the sisters began to talk about me to one another. They talked just loud enough so I could hear what they were saying. I actually felt what seemed to be knives coming through the seat into my back. As the man of God continued to speak, I could barely pay attention to what he was saying because every word the women behind were saying cut me to the core. I stayed in my seat with tears rolling down my face. God knew I wasn't strong enough to take this one. So, He intervened.

His word came to life for me right there in the midst of my furnace. The prophet called for the woman sitting on the end of the pew, the one wearing the green suit to stand up. Was he talking to me? I stood up and the man of God began to prophesy to me about what God was getting ready to do in my life. He prophesied about my ministry and the lives it would touch. He told me how God was going to bless me to own my own business and that I would be financially well off. He went on to speak into my life until I began to rejoice over what God was going to do. When I came to myself, I was on the floor worshiping at the feet of Jesus. I got up off the floor and returned to my seat. The two young ladies that were sitting behind me were no longer there. God said to me "Now where are your accusers?" It was at that moment that Psalms 23:5 became a **rhema** word for me; **(a personal revelation of the word of God that speaks directly to your situation and brings what God is saying in that scripture to life).** *"You prepare a table before me in the presence of my enemies; you anoint my head with oil; my cup runs over."* God had vindicated and blessed me right in the presence of my "enemies."

Even in the furnace, every once in a while, God would step in and cool the flames just a bit to let me know, even though you are here, I am still with you and I still love you.

God would take me out of the fire from time to time and use me to minister to someone. Then right back into the furnace I would go. God left me there until every insecurity, low self-esteem, fear, fornication, and every other stench of sin was burned up. God left me in the refiner's fire until I learned to present my body as a living sacrifice, holy and acceptable unto God. During this refining process I learned how to die and God began to live through me.

Looking for Love in All the Wrong Places

It was while in the fire that I learned what true love is. I found out that Jesus was my only true lover. He was the only one that knew me inside and out and loved me just the way I was.

While in the purification process God ministered to me about looking for love in all the wrong places. Because of the lack of affection I received as a child, I was constantly looking for a man to validate me, make me feel loved, make me feel whole.

Most of the relationships I had been in ended in the same way…rejection. The relationships that I ended were the ones that were not challenging enough for me. If the person showed me too much attention and care, that bored me. When they really did care about me, I would allow the relationship to get to a certain point and just drop it. I did not know how to love myself, so it felt strange when someone else loved me.

In the fire God began to show me myself. He showed me ugly things about me. He showed me parts of me that if anyone else ever knew they would definitely never love me. He said He loved me just the way I was, but He loved me too much to allow me to remain that way.

God used the refining fire of tests and trials to purge me of everything that was not of Him in my life. When God sends trials your way, don't fight the test. It is in the midst of the furnace that God wants to reveal Himself to you as Lord. Daniel 3: 24-25 *"Then King Nebuchadnezzar was astonished; and he rose in haste and spoke, saying to his counselors, 'Did we not cast three men bound into the midst of the fire?' They answered and said to the king, 'True, O king.' 'Look!' he answered, 'I see four men loose, walking in the midst of the fire; and they are not hurt, and the form of the fourth is like the Son of God.'"* God did not reveal Himself to Shadrach, Meshach, and Abed-Nego as Lord until they were put in the fire.

When you know him as Lord, then you can go through the fire knowing that He has everything under control (I will deal more with knowing him as Lord in the last chapter).

Chapter 7

Can We Talk?

Many of you, like me, have been looking for love in all the wrong places, but instead of love, you found rejection. I want to talk with my sisters right now, married and single…

I am a thirty-five year old single woman. I take pride in my appearance and consider myself to be well groomed and attractive. I am the last of my parents' girls to be married. I have three sisters and they are all married and raising families.

I used to hate to go to family dinners during the holidays. I loved being around my family, but I didn't like being the odd ball. You know the saying, "two is company and three is a crowd." I always felt like the third wheel. All my sisters would be there with their husband and families and then there was me. I would cry when I returned home and tell God it wasn't fair. "Why am I still single at (then) thirty-three? What is wrong with me?" is a question I often asked God. Just this year, God answered my question through a Prophet that came to minister at our church.

I had received so many prophesies concerning God sending my husband and getting married that I had reached a point where I told the Lord, "I don't want any more prophesies…Send The Prophet!" (I was referring to my husband). I didn't want to hear anymore about what God was going to do; I just wanted him to do it.

This prophecy was different however. The man of God looked right into my spirit and told me exactly what I had been asking God. He told me that I had been asking God what was wrong with me. Why am I not married yet? Then He said something that I will never forget…"God has anointed you to be alone." I thought what are you talking about. Then he went on to say that there was nothing wrong with me, but because of the anointing on my life, God had placed a hedge around me and up to that point He would not allow any man to go beyond that hedge. He said it was God that ended the other relationships. He said God was about to remove the hedge and that my husband was on the way. He told me that it was going to take a special kind of man to fill that position and to this date my standards had been set too low.

Singles, there is nothing wrong with you. God made you just the way He wanted you. And He has a time and a season for everything in your life, including your husband. When God made Eve, the first thing He did was put Adam to sleep. The reason your husband has not found you yet is because He is still sleep. When God is finished making you into the woman He is calling you to be, then He will wake your husband up. If you want God to wake up your husband, start seeking God's face. Seek His will and purpose for your life and begin to walk in it. When you delight yourself in the Lord and are complete in Him that is when the alarm clock will go off in your husband's ears.

I am now at rest with the fact that I am thirty-five and single. When God does cause my husband to find me, I will be busy fulfilling my divine purpose and not by a curbside somewhere waiting for prince charming to come by on a white horse and rescue me! Proverbs 18:22 says *"He who finds a wife finds a good thing…"* Let the man find you. Hide yourself in God and a godly man will find you!

To those who got married and thought that your husband was going to be the one to fill the empty places in your heart:

You are living with your husband, sharing the bathroom, sharing the dinner table, sharing the bed and yet you are "home alone." You want so much for him to just reach out to you. "Can't we just talk?" is a question you often ask. Your marriage has evolved into a roommate situation. You are just sharing a space and nothing more. What happened to the dreams you had? Nobody told you that marriage was going to feel this way. If only someone had told you what marriage really entailed. Marriage is not a fairy tale. Marriage is a ministry. Marriage is a commitment to another imperfect individual that constantly requires you to compromise your desires and put your spouse's needs before yours. You are feeling rejection right now. You are in this marriage, miserable and unhappy.

God sent this book to let you know that you are exactly where God wants you. God wants you to get to the place where you'll allow Him to fill the void that is in your heart. Use this time to really develop a love relationship with God. Up until now you have only known Him as Savior. He is calling you to get to know Him as Lord. The moment you allow God to be the lover of your soul and things are not going like the story book romance you dreamed of, you will still be able to rejoice because you have a lover that will love you more than any man ever could.

I speak to you now in the name of Jesus Christ and command that the spirit of rejection be loosed off of your mind. I speak hope and peace to your spirit. God is saying to you now John 14:27 *"Peace I leave with you, My peace I give to you. Let not your heart be troubled neither be afraid."* Your husband cannot give you peace like God can give it. Take a moment now and worship God and allow His peace to come in.

You may be in the furnace right now and asking God "when can I come out?" You may be saying "It's hot in here; I can't take it anymore." Be patient and wait on the Lord. Don't fight your test. Stay there until everything within you begins to say yes to the will of God.

When you die in the fire, then God will begin to live through you.

Chapter 8

The Transition…
From Rejection to Rejoicing

Death can be painful, but I recently heard a message and the speaker said, "In order to live, you have to first die but that there was life after death." As I said in the previous chapter, I learned to die while in the furnace. It was in the process of dying that I learned why I had reason to rejoice.

Your key to healing and moving from rejection to rejoicing is to die to yourself. Unless one dies first, he cannot truly live. Had Jesus not suffered the shame and rejection of the cross, He could not have experienced the resurrection. The same is true for us. Unless we take part in the suffering with Him, we cannot reign with Him. In order to get to the place of rejoicing, I had to die to my flesh.

Your flesh will say you have the right to be angry. Your flesh will say you have the right to hate the one that betrayed you, it will say, you have a right to hold a grudge and be resentful. The Bible says in Romans 8:12-13 "*Therefore, brethren, we are debtors*

- not to the flesh, to live according to the flesh. For if you live according to the flesh you will die; but if by the Spirit you put to death the deeds of the body, you will live." This is something that **you** have to do. The Bible did not say to pray that God will put to death the deeds of the flesh. The word says **you** must kill the flesh.

Renew Your Mind

The flesh is put to death when you follow Romans 8:5 "*For those who live according to the flesh set their minds on the things of the flesh, but those who live according to the Spirit, the things of the Spirit. For to be carnally minded is death, but to be spiritually minded is life and peace.*" It starts in your mind. What are you thinking about? Is your mind on who hurt you? On who betrayed you? On getting even? Romans 12:2 "*And do not be conformed to this world, but be transformed by the renewing of your mind, that you may prove what is that good and acceptable and prefect will of God.*" The only way the mind is renewed is through the word of God. Add fasting and praying and your flesh must come under subjection.

Unwanted Offspring

When rejection is planted if it is allowed to live, it will conceive and produce in your flesh unwanted offspring. Rejection will open the door to bitterness, malice, anger, hatred, envy, resentment, low self esteem, depression, and ultimately, it can lead to suicide. You must kill the seed. Pull it up by the roots before it has the chance to conceive.

While I was in the furnace, I had to go all the way back to my childhood and dig until I reached the place where rejection had first been planted.

As I said earlier, death can be painful and most likely you are experiencing pain right now. You can relate to some of my experiences because the root of rejection is still alive in you. You are hurting right now. Don't be afraid of the pain. God is trying to let you know that the seed is still alive and needs to be dealt with. It's okay to cry. God has to get us to a place where we are broken in order to administer the healing we need. Mark 14: 3 "*And being in Bethany at the house of Simon the leper, as He sat at the table, a woman came having an alabaster flask of very costly oil of spikenard. Then she broke the flask and poured it on His head.*" When you break open what is precious to you, the wall you have built to mask the pain – the boundaries you have set and dared anyone to cross – that is when God can come in and begin the healing process.

It's painful to relive our past rejections, failures, and betrayals; but if you have not dealt with the root, even though it may be buried, when the right situation comes around you will find the root of rejection sprouting up again.

I had to dig past every pain, dig past every disappointment, dig past every betrayal, dig past every blunder, dig past every insecurity, dig past what my family might say about me, and dig past what my friends thought of me. I even had to dig past what I thought of myself until I reached that ugly root of rejection, and with all the strength I had, I pulled it up and dealt with it once and for all. I killed it before it killed me. How did I kill it? Read the next chapter.

Chapter 9

WWJD...
What Would Jesus Do?

The ultimate rejection was displayed in the life of Jesus Christ. In Isaiah 53:3 *"He is despised and rejected of men, a man of sorrow and acquainted with grief. And we hid, as it were, our faces from Him; He was despised, and we did not esteem Him."* Jesus' suffering and rejection began long before the cross. In spite of His unconditional love He was constantly being rejected. Mathew 8: 28-34, *"When He had come to the other side, to the country of the Gergesenes, there met Him two demon-possessed men, coming out of the tombs, exceedingly fierce, so that no one could pass that way. And suddenly they cried out, saying, 'What have we to do with You, Jesus, You Son of God? Have You come here to torment us before out time?' Now a good way off from them there was a herd of many swine feeding. So the demons begged Him, saying, 'If You cast us out, permit us to go away into the herd of swine.' And He said to them, 'Go.' So when they came out, they went into the herd of swine. And suddenly the whole herd of swine ran violently down the steep place into the* sea, and perished in the water. Then those who kept them fled; and they went away into the city and told everything, including what had happened to the demon-possessed men. And behold, the whole city came out meet Jesus. And when they saw Him, they begged Him to depart from their region."

Jesus was rejected by His own hometown. It's one thing to be rejected, but when that rejection comes from family, the ones you least expect to betray you, it's even more devastating. Mathew 13:54-58 *"And when He had come to His own country, He taught them in their synagogue so that they were astonished and said, 'Where did this man get this wisdom and these mighty works? Is this not the carpenter's son? Is not His mother called Mary? And His brothers James, Joses, Simon, and Judas? And His sisters, are they not all with us? Where did this Man get all these things?' So that they were offended at Him. But Jesus said to them, 'A prophet is not without honor except in his own country and in his own house.' And He did not many mighty works there because of their unbelief."*

He was rejected by the multitude in Mathew 27:15-25. The same ones that were His followers, were now His accusers. They chose a notorious prisoner named Barabbas over Jesus.

Ultimately, Jesus was rejected by His Heavenly Father. Matthew 27:46 *"And about the ninth hour Jesus cried out with a loud voice, saying, 'Eli, Eli, lama sabachthani?' That is, 'My God, My God why have You forsaken me?"*

Jesus said, "Father why hast thou forsaken me?" What was Jesus' response after rejection? "Father forgive them for they no not what they do."

The root of rejection is killed by unconditional love and forgiveness.

Unconditional Love

God taught me how to love unconditionally. I loved my mother, but I had difficulty showing affection to her. Something as simple as a hug and kiss felt very uncomfortable and awkward to give. I would be afraid that it would not be received, so I just wouldn't do it.

God was going to teach me how to show love to her unconditionally. He placed my mother and I in a situation where we had to learn to communicate. We have been roommates for the past three years.

It gets difficult at times, but I am determined to defeat the enemy that tries to tell me that my mother and I will never have a normal mother and daughter relationship.

Late one night while I was praying, God instructed me to get up from my knees and go give my mother a hug and tell her that I love her. I got up my from my knees and sat on the edge of my bed. I was trying to muster up enough courage to do something that should come so easy for a daughter to share with her mother. This fear of rejection as it pertained to my mother had been taunting me for years. It would taunt me about my lack of ability to outwardly show her affection for fear that she wouldn't accept it.

I sat on the edge of my bed for about ten minutes praying in the spirit to overcome this stronghold.

It was about eleven o'clock and my mother was right outside my bedroom, ironing in the hallway. I finally rose from my bed and headed to the door, which was closed. I stopped at the door with my hand on the handle and then let go and returned to the bed. (This may seem silly to some people who have an open relationship with their parents, but I know that there are many that can relate to how I was feeling this particular night.)

When I returned to the edge of my bed, the phone rang. It was a friend who said they didn't want anything, but they just felt led to call. I shared with him what God told me to do but that it was hard and that I was afraid that mother would not receive it. He then told me that God was trying to teach me unconditional love and to get up and do what the Lord told me to do. I knew then that God wasn't playing and that if I didn't obey Him, I would miss my deliverance.

I went to my door again, but this time I opened it and went to my mother.

I gave my mother a hug (you should have seen the look on her face). I think she thought I was sick or something. I told her I loved her and asked her if she loved me. She said, "Of course I love you." Then she said, "What's wrong with you?" I said nothing was wrong but that I just wanted to know if she loved me.

I went back to my room leaving my mother with a bewildered look on her face. I cried and praised God in my bed for a while that night. I had defeated the enemy that night and the Lord said because of my obedience, He would "give me the desires of my heart." Psalms 37:4 *"Delight yourself in the Lord and He shall give you the desires of your heart."* The Hebrew word for delight in that verse is **anag, which means to be soft or pliable.** (Strong's Concordance #6026)

When you delight in the Lord by allowing your heart to become soft and pliable, then He will uphold His end and give you the desires of our heart. Surrender your heart to God. Ask Him to massage it until it becomes soft and pliable in His hands. Let Him teach you how to love unconditionally.

A few weeks later my mother came into my room one Saturday morning and serenaded me with a love song. Now, months later, she comes up to me out of the blue and gives me a kiss for no reason at all. (Yuk! smile)

When I went to give my mother a hug that night, I did not go expecting anything in return, but the return I got was far more than what I could have dreamed of.

Forgiveness

Forgiveness says, "I release you of all liability for the pain you caused me. I won't hold a grudge, I won't talk about you, I won't be bitter, and even if you choose someone over me, I won't be jealous."

I said earlier in the chapter that in order to get to the rejoicing I had to die. I had to die to my right to be bitter; I had to die to my right to be angry; I had to die to my right to be resentful. Forgiveness will take a sacrifice. Had Jesus not shed His blood on Calvary, there would be no forgiveness of sin. The Bible says in Hebrew 9:22 that without the shedding of blood there is no remission of sin.

Sacrifice

The place of sacrifice is not a pleasant place. It is a bloody place. It is a place that most people don't want to go, few of us ever get to, but all of us need to be. It is a place where pain at its highest. Leviticus 3:1-5 *"When his offering is a 'sacrifice of peace offering,' if he offers it of the herd, whether male or female, he shall offer it without blemish before the Lord. And he shall lay his hand on the head of his offering and kill it at the door of the tabernacle of meeting; and Aaron's sons, the priest, shall sprinkle the blood all around the altar. Then he shall offer from the sacrifice of the peace offering an offering made by fire to the Lord. The fat that covers the entrails and all the fat that is on the entrails, the two kidneys and the fat that is on them by the flanks, and the fatty lobe attached to the liver above the kidneys, he shall remove; and Aaron's sons shall burn it on the altar upon the burnt sacrifice, which is on the wood that is on the fire, as an offering made by fire, a sweet aroma to the Lord."* (The Hebrew word for peace means, "wholeness, completeness, soundness, health") If you want to be whole, complete, and healed, put your all on the altar of sacrifice today. There is an old hymn that asks the question, "Is your all on the altar of sacrifice laid; in your heart does the Spirit control? You will only be blessed, you'll find peace and sweet rest as you give Him your body and soul." Is your all on the altar of sacrifice? Are you willing to sacrifice your right to be angry at the one that betrayed and rejected you?

When Jesus faced rejection His response in love was, "Father forgive them for they know not what they do." Your sacrifice will involve you loving the one that rejected you. Loving the one that betrayed you. Loving the one that despitefully used you. Loving the one that molested you. Loving your mother that gave you up for adoption because you were an inconvenience. Loving your father that you never had a chance to know because he abandoned your family. Loving your babies' father that walked out on you and left you with three children to raise by yourself. For you men, loving the women that you caught with your best friend.

The love I am talking about is that Agape love. 1 Corinthians 13:4 "*Love suffers long and is kind; love does not envy; love does not parade itself, is not puffed up; does not behave rudely, does not seek its own, is not provoked, thinks no evil; does not rejoice in iniquity, but rejoices in the truth; bears all things, believes all things, hopes all things, endures all things.*"

The love that Jesus showed to us when He died for us even when we did not deserve it. No, they may not deserve your love; they may not deserve to be forgiven; they probably could care less whether you forgave them or not, but don't let that hinder you. When you sacrifice yourself through unconditional love and forgiveness it frees you, whether the other person chooses to accept it or not. The Bible says in Mathew chapter 5 to "…pray for them that hate you, revile you, say all manner of evil against you, pray and not curse." I know it hurts but that is a part of the dying. Let God complete the process. Go through; don't stop now. Allow God to show you areas that are still bleeding. Find the root, uncover it and deal with it. Dealing with it may involve going to those that hurt you and asking them to forgive you for the anger and bitterness you were holding inside.

I recently had a conversation with a pastor friend. I was sharing with him some things I had been through in the past. He stopped me and said something that caught me off guard. He told me that I needed to release certain individuals that I felt had caused me pain in the past. It caught me off guard because I thought I had already released them. I knew I had forgiven them. I knew I wasn't holding a grudge, but what was I missing? I had to do some introspection and see if there were any roots I had missed. There was, it was the root of what I thought people were thinking about me. There was still a slight bit of insecurity I would feel when I was around these individuals. I said this to say you cannot leave any roots behind. Even if it seems to be insignificant now, pull it up don't let it remain. Make sure every root is gone.

It may be painful now but remember, "Weeping may endure for a night, but joy cometh in the morning." Your morning is coming. There is life after death and your resurrection is on the way. You are right at the gate marked Rejoicing. God is completing the process of purification in you now. Let Him work on your heart in those hidden places. Ask God to give you the strength to dig up the roots of rejection that were planted so long ago. Pray with me… Father, in Jesus' name, I come before You with praise in my heart. I acknowledge that You are God and beside You there is no other. I surrender this pain to You now. I release every one that has ever rejected, abused and misused me. I give You my heart and trust You to mend every broken place. Heal me God. Heal my heart, heal my mind, heal my emotions. God, help me to love unconditionally as You have loved me. I ask that You take all of me now, every insecurity, every pain, every fear and fill me with Your glory. God let Your glory be seen in my life. Use me to bring healing to others because I have now been healed. I thank You for forgiveness as I have forgiven those who have hurt me. I lift my hands in praises and adoration to Your glorious name for You are worthy to be praised and You have made me worthy to praise You.

Now go ahead and lift up your hands in His presence. Let the tears flow. Let your praise take you into worship. Tell Him how much you love Him. Tell Him He is the center of your joy. Tell Him He is your strength. Tell Him He is your peace. Worship Him until you have released everything to Him and find rest in your spirit. You'll know when the root has died, because it is then that you will begin to rejoice…

Chapter 10

My Arrival...
Now Rejoice

I said earlier in the book that I remained in the refiner's fire for 5 years. I sat there until everything was burned up. Every once in a while (maybe three times in the whole five years) God would take me out, use me to minister to someone and put me right back in the furnace.

In April of 1998, about five years after I found out I was pregnant (five is the number of grace), God spoke to me through a sister at a Woman's Conference and said, "It is your turn now. God said this is your season." Nothing really profound, but I knew she had been sent by the Lord. I was already feeling in my spirit that I was on the verge of a great move of God in my life. I was still a member of a church that did not believe in women ministers, but God was about to do something new in my life.

The following month, I was at church one Tuesday night waiting for choir rehearsal to begin. A good friend of mine (now my Armor Bearer) and I were talking, and right in the middle of our conversation I said, "I cannot believe I have been here seven years already." Right then God spoke to me and said, "Seven is the number of completion. Your work is finished here and you are free to go."

I had been waiting for God to restore my ministry, but I did not know if He would do it there or if He would move me. Now I knew. God was moving me to another ministry. He told me I was free to go, but He didn't tell me when and where to go. I had made too many mistakes in the past by going before I was sent; so I did not make a move until I knew exactly where God was telling me to go.

I had a good relationship with my pastor, so I went to see him not many days following. I shared with him what God said but told him that I would stay there until I knew where God was telling me to go. I stayed faithful at church continuing to sing in the choir and attending Friday night Bible study.

A few weeks later my pastor was invited to preach at a church across town and the choir was to go with him. Still being faithful while waiting for God's direction, I went with the choir to this church. I had never been to this particular church before. In fact, I had never even heard of the church.

I walked into the sanctuary that night and right away my spirit felt at home. That was on a Tuesday evening. They were going to be in service the rest of the week, and I felt a pull in my spirit to go back. I went back on that Thursday, Friday and Saturday. On Saturday evening during the service God spoke to me and said, "This is the place." God had divinely ordered my steps out of the furnace and right into His purpose for my life. I joined the ministry that Sunday and preached my first message there the following Friday night. God was doing something new in me, and He was doing it in a whirlwind.

God moved in an awesome way during the service on that Friday. Long after I finished ministering that night, people were in the aisle everywhere dancing, rejoicing, and praising God for what He had done in our midst.

Joel 1:4,25-26 became another rhema word for me. "*What the chewing locust left, the swarming locust has eaten; what the swarming locust left, crawling locust has eaten; and what the crawling locust left the consuming locust had eaten. "I will restore to you the years that the swarming locust has eaten. The crawling locust. The consuming locust, the chewing locust, My great army which I sent among you. You shall eat in plenty and be satisfied. And praise the name of the Lord your God, who had dealt wondrously with you; and My people shall know that I am in the midst of Israel: I am the Lord your God and there is no other. My people shall never be put shame.*"

During those five years in the refiner's fire, it seemed as though everything had been eaten up around me. My friends were few. I went from being self-supporting to actually relying on public assistance for a period of about nine months to make it. I wasn't being called to minister anywhere. But from that Friday night on, God has been working miracles in my life and my ministry. He then brought the scripture you just read to my mind and said "don't worry about the time you think you have lost while in the fire these past five years, for I will restore unto you the years that the locust have eaten."

I am not saying that I don't at times still feel rejection. What has happened is I have changed the way I handle rejection now. I realized that it's not what happens to me that determines my outcome, but it's how I handle what happens to me that will either produce a victim or a victor. And I refuse to be a victim any longer, for I am more than a conqueror!

Chapter 11

Rejoice, Even Through The Pain

When you know Jesus as Lord and place your life in His hands trusting Him to do His perfect will, you may have to rejoice through the pain at times.

A year or so ago I was in a relationship that I thought would end in marriage. We had discussed colors, how many would be in the wedding party, the time of day the wedding would take place and so on. I just knew he was "the one." During a conversation we were having, I was informed that I, however, was not "the one." He said the relationship wasn't working, and he didn't want to pursue it any longer. This time, because I had already come out of the fire and pulled up the roots of rejection, when the rejection tried to conceive, it found nothing to feed on. Don't get me wrong, I was hurt, but this time I handled the rejection differently.

One evening I was in my room and I felt in my spirit the urgency to get into the presence of the Lord. I was still hurting from the break up and I felt God wanted to do something for me that night. I got down on my knees and began to give God praise. (**When I pray I never start right off with my petitions, I always begin with praise and thanksgiving, the Bible says to enter into His gates with thanksgiving and into His courts with praise**).

There I was on my knees praising God, when God began to speak to me. He told me to pray for this man who had recently ended our relationship. I did what the Lord instructed me to do. I did not pray for God to bring him back into my life. I prayed for his ministry; I prayed for God's will to be done in his life; I prayed for his job, his finances, whatever God brought to my mind, I prayed for. I finished praying a few minutes later and started to get up from my knees, God spoke and said, " Now pray for his wife." I said, "What do you mean pray for his wife?" He said, "Pray for the wife that I am preparing for him." I said "God, that hurts. I thought I was going to be his wife, and You are telling me to pray for the one that You are preparing for him." God then said, "How much do you love me? Yes, the heart of the king is in my hand, and I could touch his heart and turn it back to you, but I want to know, how much do you love me? Are you willing to sacrifice the promise for me?" He then reminded me of the story of Abraham and Isaac...

(Genesis 18:10) *"And He said, 'I will certainly return to you according to the time of life, and behold, Sarah your wife shall have a son.* (21:1-3) *And the Lord visited Sarah as He had said, and the Lord did for Sarah as He had spoken. For Sarah conceived and bore Abraham a son in his old age, at the set time which God had spoken to him. And Abraham called the name of his son who was born to him – whom Sarah bore to him – Isaac.* (22:1-12) *Now it came to pass after these things that God tested Abraham, and said to him, 'Abraham!' And he said, 'Here I am.' And He said, 'Take now your son, your only son Issac, whom you love, and go to the land of Moriah, and offer him there as a burnt offering on one of the moun-*

tains of which I shall tell you.' So Abraham rose early in the morning and saddled his donkey and took two of his young men with him, and Isaac his son; and he split the wood for the burnt offering, and arose and went to the place which God had told him. Then on the third day Abraham lifted his eyes and saw the place afar off. And Abraham said to his young men, 'Stay here with the donkey; the lad and I will go yonder and worship, and will come back to you.' So Abraham took the wood of the burnt offering and laid it on Isaac his son; and he took the fire in his hand, and a knife, and the two of them went together. But Isaac spoke to Abraham his father and said, 'My father!' And he said, 'Here I am, my son.' And he said, 'Look, the fire and the wood, but where is the lamb for a burnt offering?' And Abraham said, 'My son, God will provide for Himself the lamb for a burnt offering.' And the two of them went together. Then they came to the place of which God had told him. And Abraham built an altar there and placed the wood in order; and he bound Isaac his son and laid him on the altar, upon the wood. And Abraham stretched out his hand and took the knife to slay his son. But the Angel of the Lord called to him from heaven and said, 'Abraham, Abraham!' And he said, 'Here I am.' And He said, 'Do not lay your hand on the lad, or do anything to him; for I now know that you fear God, since you have not withheld your son, *your only son from me."* The term fear means to hold God in awe. **(notice Abraham never questioned God; when God spoke, he just obeyed)**

Abraham loved God so much that he was willing to sacrifice the very promise that God had given him. I can see Abraham walking up that mountain to the place of sacrifice with tears rolling down his face. He was probably playing back all of the precious moments he had spent watching his son grow up, the son that he had waited twenty-five years for God to bring. And now that Isaac was there, God asked Abraham to sacrifice the one thing that meant the world to him.

What are you willing to give up to the Lord? If God said for you to let it go today, would you? That night I let my dream go. I let the promise of becoming a bride go as I began to pray for the woman who would one day marry the man I thought I was going to marry. I prayed a fervent prayer. You would have thought I was praying for a special loved one. I prayed that God would bless her, whoever she was. I prayed for God to instill in her everything that she needed to please the one he was preparing her for. I prayed for her ministry (just in case she was in ministry). I prayed that God would supply her every need. I prayed and prayed until God said, " Well done." When I finished praying for her I fell prostrate on my face. Then God spoke to me and said, "Now, that is worship." I had died to my desires and to my way, and when I died, my sacrifice led me "beyond the veil[1]" and right into the very presence of God.

Not only will your sacrifice kill the roots of rejection, but it will lead you to a place of worship that you never imagined. That night I could hear the voice of Jesus in Gethsemane so clear…"Not my will but thine will be done."

I felt so close to my Lord and Savior that I just rested there on the floor lying at His feet. When I finally did get up, I got up with praise in my heart. I danced around my room and rejoiced because I had been in my Savior's presence and my heart that had been broken before I began to pray, was now healed!

God is showing you something right now that He has been telling you to let go of. You know that relationship is not good for you. You have stopped praying and studying your word. You have allowed that relationship to consume you and push God to the back burner. Return to your first love. Let God take you back to that place where you first believed him. Trust God, give it up and He will do more for you than that relationship ever could.

---

[1]I am currently working on my next book entitled "Beyond the Veil, Another Dimension of Worship."

I break soul ties right now in the name of the Lord Jesus Christ. I command you to loose that woman. You will loose that man and let them go. I speak to the spirit of compromise that is trying to make you believe that you can't live without that man and I command it to flee! I plead the blood of Jesus over your mind, over your emotions, over your spirit and I declare and decree your victory! Start praising God right where you are. Praise Him for your liberty. Praise Him for your freedom. Whom the Son sets free is free indeed! And be not again entangled in the yoke of bondage. **Don't go back.** I don't care how much he begs and pleads. If the relationship was of God, it would have added to your spiritual life not robbed you of it.

Chapter 12

Rejoice in the Lord, and Again, I Say Rejoice!

I said earlier in the book when you have Jesus as Lord, you can go through the fire knowing that Jesus has everything in control.

Phil 3:10 "*That I may know Him in the power of His resurrection, and the fellowship of His sufferings…*" You come to know Jesus as Lord when you fellowship with Him in His suffering. That is why you have felt the sting of rejection so. When you told the Lord you wanted a personal relationship with Him, you set yourself up for rejection. We read earlier how Jesus suffered rejection. If He suffered rejection and you want to know Him, then the only way to know Him is to fellowship in His suffering. He was rejected; so you too must be rejected. So, rather then have a pity party over the one who deserted you, you need to go back to them and say thank you. Because it was when they left you that your fellowship with Jesus began. Rejoice!

Rejoice In Knowing Adoni

One of the Hebrew words for Lord is *adown, pronounced "aw-done" :* mean. To *rule; sovereign, i.e. controller (human or divine): -lord, master, owner.*

When you know Jesus as "Adoni" or Lord, then you can rejoice despite what comes your way. You can rejoice in the face of rejection, death, sickness, heartache or persecution because you know that "Adoni" is sovereign and controller and nothing that comes into your life can come except He allow it.

Psalms 139:16 says *"Your eyes saw my substance, being yet unformed. And in Your book they were all written, the days fashioned for me, when as yet there were none of them."* Nothing that has happened to you was a surprise to God. Even the days yet to come, God already knows. God knew that if He allowed you to be rejected long enough, it would draw you into His arms. If He allowed you to be rejected enough times, then you would intensify your prayer life. You can rejoice in the fact that if God allows it, it must be for your good. It may hurt right now, but it has to work for your good because of Romans 8:28 *"And we **know**, all things work together for good to those who love God, to those who are the called according to His purpose."* So, rejection has to work for your good. Heartache has to work for your good. Betrayal has to work for your good. That is why what was supposed to kill you or make you lose your mind didn't work. Give yourself a high five and say, "I'm still here!" Rejoice! The enemy meant it for evil against you, but God meant it for your good. When the enemy tried to kill you, it just caused you to pray more. When he tried to make you lose your mind, you developed a hunger and thirst after righteousness.

Many people have been through the same things that you and I have been through but never made it out. They ended up committing suicide or in a padded cell somewhere. Rejoice because you survived what was supposed to be your demise. Do you remember that old song, "I will survive?" Tell the enemy, "You thought it would destroy me, but I will survive. Did you think I would crumble? Did you think I would just lay down and die? Oh no, not I. I have survived!" Just think about all that you have been through and all that you survived. When I think about all that I have been through and survived to tell, I can't help but enter into uninhibited Worship. When the roots of rejection are gone…..Rejoicing becomes automatic!

Jesus and Jesus Alone

There is only one person that you can put your complete trust in and know that He will never reject you, Jesus and Jesus alone. He said in His word, "I will never leave you nor will I forsake you. Lo I am with you always, even until the end of the earth." Man will fail you. People will love you one day and hate you the next. Jesus is the same Yesterday, Today and Forever. He will never change on you.

NOW THAT IS REASON TO REJOICE!!!

*H*ere are some additional scriptures that will strengthen and encourage you during your process from Rejection to Rejoicing:

Psalms 34:17-18

The righteous cry out, and the Lord hears, and delivers them out of all their troubles. The Lord is near to those who have a broken heart,
And saves such as have a contrite spirit (crushed in spirit).

Psalm 31:1-2

In You, O Lord, I put my trust; Let me never be ashamed; Deliver me in Your righteousness. Bow down Your ear to me, Deliver me speedily, A fortress of defense to save me.

Psalms 147:1-3

Praise the Lord! For it is good to sing praises to our God; for it is pleasant; and praise is beautiful. The Lord builds up Jerusalem; He gathers together the outcasts of Israel. He heals the broken-hearted
And binds up their wounds.

Isaiah 53:4

Surely He has borne our griefs and carried our sorrows;
Yet we esteemed Him stricken Smitten by God, and afflicted.
But, He was wounded for our transgressions, He was bruised for our iniquities the chastisement of our peace was upon Him, And by His stripes we are healed.

Matthew 5:43-44

"You have heard that it was said, 'You shall love your neighbor and hate your enemy.' But I say to you, love your enemies, bless those who curse you, do good to those who hate you, and pray for those who spitefully use you and persecute you…

John 14:27

"Peace I leave with you, My peace I give to you; not as the world gives do I give to you. Let not your heart be troubled, neither let it be afraid.

Ephesians 6:10

Finally, my brethren, be strong in the Lord and in the power of His might. Put on the whole armor of God, that you may be able to stand against the wiles of the devil.

2 Corinthians 12:9

And He said to me, "My grace is sufficient for you, for My strength is made perfect in weakness." Therefore most gladly I will rather boast in my infirmities that the power of Christ may rest upon me. Therefore I take pleasure in infirmities, in reproaches, in needs, in persecutions, in distresses, for when I am weak, then I am strong.

Philippians 4:6

Be anxious for nothing, but in everything by prayer and supplication, with thanksgiving, let your request be made know to God; and the peace of God, which surpasses all understanding, will guard your hearts and minds through Christ Jesus. Finally, brethren, whatever things are true, whatever things are noble, whatever things are just, whatever things are pure, whatever things are lovely, whatever things are of good report, if there be any virtue if there be anything praiseworthy-meditate on these things.

CPSIA information can be obtained at www.ICGtesting.com
Printed in the USA
LVOW081809040212

267067LV00001B/18/A